Now and Then

poems by
Robert A. Shearer

STEPHEN F. AUSTIN STATE UNIVERSITY PRESS

Production Manager: Kimberly Verhines
Front Cover Art: Anete Lusina via Pexels.com

IBSN: 978-1-62288-952-5

For more information:
Stephen F. Austin State University Press
P.O. Box 13007 SFA Station
Nacogdoches, Texas 75962
sfapress@sfasu.edu
www.sfasu.edu/sfapress
936-468-1078

Distributed by Texas A&M University Press Consortium

Dedicated to

Pauline Kremenak Shearer

Also by Robert A. Shearer

Interviewing: Theories, Techniques, and Practices (2005)

Swift (2014)

Port Sullivan (2016)

Attack On the SPORTPLATZ (2016)

Songs Of the Warriors (2017)

Contents

Preface

Now and Then is an anthology of original compositions written over the last five years. Nevertheless, they represent a lifetime of personal and private experiences, insights, ideas, and impressions. The poems represent, strong or weak, a serious first attempt to share these very personal expressions with others. Writing them was a creative exploration and immersion for a person with dubious, unpromising, and unexpected scholarly origins.

The title of the book is meant to convey two meanings. First, the title reflects the occasional nature of the creation of the poems as inspiration occurred. They were written, triggered, and driven by inspiration. The writing didn't follow a preset schedule, timeline, or calendar. So, they were written at various times and in various places, because, as most writers and artists know, inspiration is frequently unexpected, serendipitous, and fleeting. Second, the title conveys the content of the poems from a temporal perspective. Some of the poems contain historical content, "then," while others contain rather contemporary themes or current events occurring "now."

The contents of the book are divided into five parts: Historical Poems, Philosophical Poems, Humorous Poems, Mythical Poems, and Social Commentary Poems. Within the five parts, a diverse number of subjects are featured including: Campus unrest in the '60s, portable potties, mythical beasts, rat ranches, cryptids, coronavirus, and mountain bikes. In these five parts, the reader will likely find haunting, satirical, realistic, and metaphorical themes. Admittedly, some of the poems could have been located in multiple parts of the book and the reader may think the poem should have appeared in a different part, fait accompli.

Finally, the anthology could be divided into poems that tell a story and poems that comment on contemporary observations, events, or trends. But, the distinctions and classifications didn't seem as thematically clear as the parts that were chosen for the contents of the anthology.

How were these poems written? In these poems, the process of creating and writing the poems typically followed a six-step sequence.

First, there had to be an experience of an inspirational moment or vision. This experience has been referred to as "pictures in the mind." In the case of poems, it would be "words in the mind." In other words, some external event or observation triggers a stimulus that leads to a visualization of how a poem might be formed. These words can come and go quite quickly and be difficult to retrieve after a busy day starts. They occur often in the strange mental kaleidoscope zone upon waking up in the morning or right before falling asleep at night, so I sometimes keep a pen and notepad by the bed so that visualized poetic words and pictures were not lost.

Second, the gestalt of the poem was formed by visualizing the title and the first verse in my mind, or, if it was a brief poem, the entire poem. This was the aha and viola moment in the inspiration. Third, a quick rough draft of the poem was produced by free association. The goal of this step was to get the coalescing gestalt on paper before any ideas or initial details were forgotten. This cognitive phenomenon of retroactive inhibition can occur when later visions hinder the memory of faint earlier visions. Whatever the case, this was the "brain-to-pen-to-paper" word processing step. At this point, writing the poem and pushing toward a finished product became a near obsession and tour de force.

Fourth, the poem was rewritten and "scrubbed" a little for a clean-up of the original outpouring of the verses. This step frequently consisted of multiple rewriting versions and rearrangement of the verses. Fifth, the poem was re-rhymed if any rhyming sequences needed to be improved. The goal of this step was to make the rhyming in the verse as smooth and as flowing as possible so that the rhyming didn't appear to be haphazardly or crudely contrived. The goal was to make the rhyming in the poem almost unnoticed. Between the fourth and sixth steps, the poem was set aside for a day or two before being reread and potentially changed.

Sixth, the final version of the poem was written. The task of this step was to achieve a delicate balance of the final rewriting without risking overwriting, correcting, and editing the poem. Unfortunately, without the initial inspiration, the subsequent steps are meaningless or futile and not likely to produce a poem. Inspiration is the genesis of the process.

All of the poems in this anthology were created and written by me. They may represent a small portion of my existential beliefs, worldly perceptions, sense of humor, and philosophy of life. Taken as a whole or individually, the poems are my responsibility, so I am responsible for their content. Any mistakes, omissions, indiscretions, missteps, or errors are mine. Any acclaim and recognition for the anthology will be reserved for a later date.

I consider myself an experienced writer and raconteur, having written and published several books, but I fully realize that I am a novice poet. Hopefully, this lack of experience will not reduce any satisfaction, enjoyment, and eustress that you have reading the poems, now and then.

Robert A. Shearer: 7-8-11

Humor

The Thicket Cricket

There once was a chirping cricket who lived in a thicket,
Whose chirper suddenly went awry.
He frantically rubbed his wings together,
But couldn't make a sound even though he continued to try.

If he didn't chirp in the thicket,
So that the other crickets could hear,
His chirping song would disappear,
And they wouldn't know he was near.

He first asked a grasshopper who lived in the thicket
If he knew what he should do.
The grasshopper said he didn't know,
Because all grasshoppers do is hop and chew.

Next, he asked the cockroach, who lived there also,
How to make his chirping glorious and effusive.
The cockroach also said he didn't know,
Because cockroaches are only silent and elusive.

He then said to the spider,
"My music has left me, alas and alack."
The spider also said she didn't know what to do,
Because spiders only spin webs to catch their next snack.

Finally, he asked and old cricket what he should do.
The old cricket knew immediately what was wrong.
"Put the bottom wing over the top wing so that the top is on the
bottom."
The cricket changed the wings and started chirping a glorious song.

Black Poodle In a White Renegade

A black poodle sat up high and stately in the seat
Of a monster-wheeled white Renegade,
Showing a poodle's mystique, prestige, and conceit.
This pampered pooch is poised for a gnarly off-road escapade.

Coal black eyes and curly coat,
Skinny legs and feet,
This Renegade canine
Is very proud and elite.

No Wrangler or Sahara for this pup,
Because he wants all the SUV accessories
For a Renegade that is tricked out and gussied-up.
Woof-woof, he rocks the tube doors, rhino bumpers, and lift kits.

What an amazing duo, this chic pup and jeep,
And an unlikely sight to see on an esplanade.
But they can cruise any trail regardless of how rough or steep,
A black poodle in a white Renegade.

E Mountain Bikes

Buying an E bike will take a large amount of money out of your pocket,
Take you whizzing down the road with electric assist,
And give you a spark and a kick in your sprocket,
So that you transform into an electrified wizard.

You can ride 'em on the trail with tires that are fat and knobby,
But you'll get a mouth full of mud or dirt
If you are unseated because you're unsteady or wobbly,
And become a careening, wheeling, and helmeted dervish.

An E bike is not a scooter or a moped,
Or a Harley, Moto Guzzi, or a Honda either.
It's a high tech, boosted, and zapped velocipede,
That will, upon contact with a car, send you catapulted into the ether.

You can have your Segways, electric skateboards, and electric pogos.
It's full suspension us big boys like,
With fat bodies, fat tires, and fat egos.
We need an E mountain bike to send us wheeling down the pike.

The Skinny Steed

A farmer went to the livestock auction
To buy a horse to ride across the prairie
After transacting a horse adoption.
After all, what is a farm without a horse?

The farm was a hobby
And he didn't know much about farming.
He was also a newbie,
Not knowing much about horses.

He fed the new horse well,
But the horse got skinnier and skinnier
As anyone could tell.
Bones began to show as the horse got thinner.

The horse had been cheap
And older than most,
But he didn't want it to die in a heap,
So, he called a skinny horse expert.

The expert said, "This is profound.
This skinny steed has no teeth,
And all of the food you've fed has fallen on the ground.
This is truly a poorly nag."

The farmer was aghast,
That he had bought such a horse
And watched it decline so fast.
He had failed to look in the horse's mouth.

He'd ridden across the plain
On a poor old toothless nag,
Who was terminally skinny and losing its tail and mane,
And who was destined soon for a dog food bag.

4 X 4

You can cruise it around
The shopping mall parking lot,
Or take it to a food truck
To get a tasty taco or nacho.

After all, you have to show-off
The 4x4 truck that you bought.
An AWD is for a fuddy-duddy
As well is a 4x2 knockoff.

You gotta have a 4x4
That is mega macho
And an off-road beast
That doodle buggers adore.

But, whatever you do,
And wherever you go,
There is a very important cue:
Don't get it muddy.

Bow Wow Boosters

If you wanna keep your dog safe and secure,
You have to put 'em in a car seat
To ensure that the dog is haute couture
And buckled up for canine safety.

If your fur baby is rambunctious and frisky,
Riding him in the back of an open truck
Is, with a sudden stop, dangerous and risky
Because if he flies out, he will be surely struck.

You can strap in your loveable Labrador,
To keep your furry pet from flying
Or hurling through the windshield or open door,
So that your pooch won't be dog gone.

If you want to protect your perky poodle,
Put her in a doggie car seat and chill
So, if your car does a dipsy-doodle,
Your poodle won't become high-priced road kill.

Buckle up your hyper hound inside the truck
So, if your truck hits another truck
Your hound doesn't become a dead duck,
And you wished you had installed a pet car seat.

You can ride your lanky Great Dane in a Cadillac,
But if the caddy careens into a crash,
And the unsecured big boy breaks his sacroiliac,
The doggie doctor will get a lot of your cash.

Show off your BFF bulldog in a Honda Civic,
And give the friendly pup a lift.
But, the ride could be horrific
If your stout pup isn't strapped in.

Take a trip with your feisty, pint-sized Chihuahua
In a dually four-by-four truck
All the way up to Alaska or down to Baja
Snapped into a tiny pet booster seat.

Your primped and prissy Pekingese
Will feel right at home strapped in a Rubicon,
And will enjoy the ride with seeming ease
Protected from vehicular harm in a doggie seat.

No matter the number of dogs, one-to-five,
A bow wow booster
Will keep them safe and alive
To ride another day.

Phat Cat

Behold the prowling refined feline
Who, a meal, would never decline.
It might be quite rude
To attribute his girth to food,
Because this phat cat is fur baby fine.

This quite lithe and refined city kitty
Looks like he was designed by a committee.
He's part rescue Siamese,
And other breeds, if you please.
In appearance, this phat cat is mottled quite pretty.

Many people prefer dogs over cats for pets,
And many others like lizards or snakes, with few regrets.
But if you're looking for a dreamy,
Furry, and stealthy affection queenie,
This phat cat is as good as it gets.

Yum Sayin?

It seems our speech has become afflicted with filleritus,
Like, yum sayin?
When will the crutch words go away?
Like, yum askin?
Please delete the gobbledygook and word salad.
Like, yum prayin?
Slower, clearer, and uncluttered speech please.
Like, yum rockin?

OFFF

If you go to Mickey D's during morning coffee time,
You will likely find a group of bodacious Old Farts Finding Fault,
Drinking coffee and jawing about the national decline.
Their collective wisdom, they will readily exalt.

For this group, no pancakes, eggs, or sausages,
Because it's the senior coffee rate with a free refill
To warm the pipes of these astute sages
So, they can find fault unrestricted and at will.

This group finds fault with political, economic, and sports trends
With hearty grousings, grumblings, and gripes.
But, these precious elders, relatives, and friends
Are a generational treasure because they have earned their stripes.

So, if you pop into a Mickey D's some morning,
Smile when you spot the Old Farts Finding Fault
But heed this friendly warning:
Please take their comments with a grain of salt.

Ole Bucky

The game warden placed in plain sight a plastic decoy deer named Bucky.
He wanted to catch illegal shooting from the road into a farmer's field
By armed and trigger-happy dirt road scofflaws
    who thought they'd gotten lucky.
He hid and waited to see how many violators his clever ploy would yield
When, unsuspecting, they drove by, stopped and shot ole Bucky down.

Ole Bucky, filled with foam, stood in the field with a fixed stare
And eight-point antlers held high to the sky,
Beckoning an unsuspecting poacher to shoot if he dare.
He wagged his mechanical tail held high,
Signaling to a hunter to c'mon and shoot ole Bucky down.

Several yahoos who had been smoking pot
And riding four-wheelers on a trail
Blasted the clever imposter with a load of buckshot.
Their devil-may-care salvo was to no avail
As they riddled ole Bucky and shot him down.

A goat roper in a pick-em-up truck
Couldn't resist a shooting temptation.
With buck fever, he fired many bullets at the stuffed buck,
And now he's facing harsh incarceration
Because he blasted away and shot ole Bucky down.

A city slicker out for a morning drive
Spotted the decoy in the prominent location.
Not suspecting the deer wasn't alive, blasted it with his 45.
Now he's facing losing many bucks after his hefty citation
Because he was hoodwinked when he shot ole Bucky down.

A local banker was on a brief journey
To look at some foreclosed property.
He's now looking for a defense attorney
Because he discharged his gun improperly
When he, from the road, potshot ole Bucky down.

Ole Bucky has lost one eye
And one of the antlers in his rack,
But this plastic faux buck just won't die.
After many a bushwhacking attack,
He's still ready for a poacher to shoot ole Bucky down.

Now ole Bucky lays on the groun'
Looking like Swiss cheese, shredded and perforated
And the perps are in the hoosegow in town
After being charged and waiting to be prosecuted
'Cause they shot ole Bucky down.

Purple Worm Eaters

In case you haven't noticed or observed,
There seems to be an endless array
Of plastic fishing worms that are colored
For catching finicky finny fishes in a stream, lake, or bay.

The wiggly scriggly fishing fakes
Come in red, blue, black, green, and pink,
And are a staple of tackle boxes on all the lakes.
What must a worker at a Chinese worm factory think?

In the US, are there no free worms in the ground
To be skewered on a hook that is sharp
And then cast into water to be drowned
As a bait to trick an unsuspecting catfish or carp?

Are there fish that eat purple worms in the USA?
And, are the fish that shrewd and discriminating
As they swim the deeps and shallows looking for prey?
The US has finicky purple worm eaters. How amazing!

The Yellow Dillo

The little armored creature with nine bands
Roams the vast llano around Amarillo
And digs and burrows in the woodlands.
She is a yellow dillo, among mostly gray dillos,
Which is a rare and striking trait for armadillos.
This dandy dillo, named Sasparilla,
Is very good at smelling and hearing,
But her vision is not so keen,
As she forages under the mesquites and willows
For grubs, beetles, and catipilla's.
Among her species, she is special and unique
And her amarillo coloration scheme
Provides an amazing and beautiful mystique
For the Yellow Dillo on the llano scene.

Sundi

There once was a rescued coatimundi
Who was given the name Sundi.
He's not a squirrel, coon, or ringtail with a long nose,
But looks a bit like all of those.
He is a rambunctious, tree-climbing, and spry guy.

Sundi's wild family lives in warmer climes
And is found in South Texas and Arizona, sometimes.
They eat grubs, beetles, and termites they expose,
Sniffing them out with their long nose.
Do coatimundis make good pets? No times!

Philosophy

Dancing To Forget

Forgetting.
Remembering.
Forgetting to forget.
Remembering and fretting.
Remembering to forget.

Memory invasions from the past,
Suppressed and repressed,
Ooze from the icky preconscious darkness,
And leave us horribly aghast and obsessed.
Even so, we do the dance to forget.

As we get older yet,
And as more dead rats get caught
In our memory trap,
It gets harder to forget.
Sadly, age creates a greater struggle and desperate need
To dance to keep from remembering.

Erotic specters that dance furtively
In and out of consciousness,
Create a dancing ambivalence
That pricks and haunts the conscience.
Undaunted, we keep dancing futilely.

Joyful memories have sadly faded
Under the weight of time, stress, and pain,
And drifted away like zephyrs in the memory.
Forgetting whisks the joy away, numbs our brain,
And overwhelms, as we dance to forget.

Riding the Green Line

Pathfinding with the ever-changing kaleidoscope of Color Weather Radar
Can make a cyclist's ride a fair-weather dream,
And the challenge is to deftly navigate the droning spinning wheels
Outside the warning of the undulating green seam.
Inside the green, the knobby, spinning tires will spit the pebbles
    and spray the water
In your face and up your front and back,
'Cause on a bicycle there ain't no fenders or wipers, jack.

So, ride the green line
And the weather will be fine.

Riding the green line is time spent
That will make your ride quite sublime.
If you carefully heed the colorful digital display,
CWR will help your ride be a grand ole time.
Light or dark green, outside the green line is a cyclist's safe path.
But, crossing the green line can put a fair-weather rider
At the mercy of the pesky precipt puddles and nature's wrath.

Ride the green line
And you will feel safe, dry, and divine.

Leaving the green and crossing into the yellow patterns
Can be a torrential kamikaze miscalculation,
So, when it happens, you might need to find some overhead protection.
Yellow hues and designs indicate moderate rain on the plain.
So, wipe your goggles, don your togs, and ride hell-bent for cover.
If not, the rain will become your drenching bane.

So, following the CWR and riding the green line
Will give you the safe and dry sign.

If you ride across the orange line,
You have strayed much too far.

The rain will be heavy, swirling, and relentless,
And you will wish you were riding in a comfy compact car.
You will look and feel like a drowned road rat.
The piercing wind will be blowing, the bike will be heaving,
And it will be too late to escape, retreat, or scat.

So, ride the green line,
And you'll likely stay dry by design.

To escape the danger and fury of the red line,
You'll have to desperately peddle rapidly,
Or be riding a drag bike or a crotch rocket,
But all you have is your puny legs and a chain around a sprocket.
Riding the red line will not only get you buffeted and soaked,
But also, if lightning strikes you or your bike,
You'll probably be crispy, combusted, or croaked.

So, if the radar turns red,
Don't be a dum-dum or knucklehead.
You need to skedaddle, run for cover,
     save your lightly helmeted phat head,
And get the hell off the velocipede.

Neanderthals In Heaven?

Will there be Neanderthals in heaven,
Gallivanting around the streets of gold
With our other ancient departed brethren?
Will they be tall or short, young or old?

Will we get an introduction to a *homo erectus* lady,
Or meet the children of a *Denisovan* tribe,
Who flourished during their heyday,
But have now become a DNA ascribe?

Will we discover that *homo sapiens*
Who inhabit the earth today,
Came as ancient aliens
While all of the other species faded away?

Will we attend a party with *homo naledi* or *nabilis*
Who walked the land long ago
And left stones, bones, and DNA for analysis
So their characteristics we might know?

If and when we get to paradise,
Will there be Neanderthals there,
And will we learn of their demise,
And the destiny of *homo sapiens*, if we dare?

Cypress Creek

On a stream branch off the mighty Tennessee
I wooed a lovely appealing southern lady,
Who, in my mind's eye, was quite unique,
On the bank of picturesque and serene Cypress Creek.

She lived on the bluffs above the mighty river,
And in the moonlight, her eyes would dance and quiver.
My imagination ran wild, as her affection I did seek
On the shady enchanted bank of Cypress Creek.

The rushing water of the river made eddies and swirls
And reminded me she wasn't like other girls,
Even though I'd only known her a week,
As we parked in the car above the bank of Cypress Creek.

When the creek caressed the river, it made dancing whirlpools.
When I was with her, I felt like all the other fools,
Their heads spinning like the pools, who could barely speak
While wishing they could see her on the bank of Cypress Creek.

Cypress Creek intersected the river after originating far to the north.
After snaking to the south, it's dark green water slowly poured forth.
The bluffs across the river from our retreat were rugged, rocky, and bleak,
But my infatuation was focused on the lady at Cypress Creek.

The mighty Tennessee ran deep, swift, and wide,
Its journey to the west to the Mississippi not to be denied.
But I was on a different journey, trapped by her sensuous mystique
Like the mesmerizing undercurrent at the confluence of Cypress Creek.

The white shells of the ancient occupational mounds sparkled in the sunlight
And signaled this had been, for thousands of years, a sweet home site.
Her demure signaled a sweet home and inviting stylish chic,
As sweet as the muscadines hanging from the trees over Cypress Creek.

On the creek bank intersecting the mighty Tennessee,
I kissed a lady with wild abandonment and esprit,
Who was a young man's captivating dream
On the idyllic bank of that Cypress stream.

Social Commentary

Rancho de Ratas

Yippee ki-yay! The rats are on a ranch,
Being wrangled as micro-livestock for sale.
Yes, these furry little trap familiars
Are being raised in colonies on a large scale.

These gnawing agri-vermin
Are socially protected and upwardly mobile
Because of this ratty micro-farmin'
And an increasing demand for tasty rats.

These eeky aristocratic gnawers,
Nourished, pampered and indulged,
Are the cash yielding residential top drawers
Of an agri-grow vermin operation.

But, alas, these well fed, cheese gobblin' long tails
Become meaty snacks for sanctuary raptors and reptiles,
After being euthanized, shrink wrapped, and frozen for agri-sales.
A bon chat, bon rat.

Horse Busses

You can load two horses, four, six, or eight.
You can even load nags, cow ponies, and thoroughbreds
Into a fancy silver trailer for equine freight.
This bus for horses is a pretentious equestrian luxury ride.

So, we haul 'em to the horse show or arena to promenade,
Where we can briefly, on them, ride astride.
After they ride on us in a cross-country bus cavalcade,
We say, "giddy-up" to clip-clopping aristocratic beasts.

Whoa to busses like Greyhounds and Trailways.
These primped, perfumed, and pampered steeds
Travel the highways and byways
In horse busses of barnyard opulence and chic.

From the pasture, bring on the mules and jennies.
Load 'em in the roomy hitched up horse bus,
That costs an equestrian some pretty pennies.
How pastoral is the sound of he-haws and brays coming from the bus?

A horse bus shouldn't be used to carry goats or sheep:
It just isn't kosher, comely, or cowboy.
Anyway, smaller animals don't know they are going first class.
It makes the pricey horse bus look tacky, kitsch, and cheap.

Worse, hauling chickens would be absolutely foul.
Feathers flying from a horse bus would be a ghastly sight,
And, their coup poop would deliver a malodorous smell from the fowl.
So, it's horse feathers to these preening, pungent, poultry passengers.

Now, these big saddled quadrupedal pets have the upper hoof.
After thousands of years as beasts of burden,
They now ride with windows, air conditioning, and a protective roof.
Maybe horses got their wishes.

Free the Coronials

The inconvenient, intractable, insidious, and deadly Covid
Has thrown a stifling lid
Over our social, religious, and occupational activities,
And thwarted our usual proclivities.

Now, we're whining and having a fit,
Sitting and suffering in this pity pie pot,
Not being able
To do diddly-squat.

Is it a plague, scourge, or apocalypse?
Few seem to know.
While we sit and fiddle and chafe at the restrictions,
The tally of death and suffering continues to grow.

Some say it's a hoax and we've been scammed
And have acted with mass hysteria.
So, the Covid be damned
As they rush to freedom and mobility.

The authorities recommend respiratory protection
To keep us out of the ICU.
But new cases move in the upward direction,
Because the carrier could be me and you.

But the denied viral sickness
Without a vaxx, uncontained, and unseen
Moves with deadly quickness
As we frantically spray, disinfect, and clean.

So away with the masks, house arrests, and social distancing (SD).
We wanna be free,
Maybe if only to a small degree.
Cooped up Coronials gotta be free.

Truck Nutz

You can swing 'em from your duallie's hitch
Or hang 'em from the bumper of your four-by-four.
Either way, they're truly scrotal cowboy kitsch,
As your Truck Nutz go flying in the wind.

You can adorn the back of your Dodge hemi,
Or spiff-up your Ford Predator,
Or adorn your GMC Jimmy
As your Truck Nutz gather dust going down the road.

You don't have a macho Renegade,
Wrangler, or Rubicon
If you take your neutered Jeep up a steep grade
Without Truck Nutz torquing in the wind.

Truck Nutz are not for a Tesla or Lexus.
They would also drag in the mud on an Infinity or Mercedes,
But you can wire 'em to a Titan as a bovine nexus.
You gotta keep Truck Nutz hanging high.

Old or new truck, empty or full tank, diesel or gas fuel,
Ya gotta have trashy testicular trappings
If you want a pick-em-up that is super duty cool.
Only Truck Nutz can convey visceral pizzazz dangling in the wind.

Electric, four cylinders, six, or eight,
A truck on a rutted back road deserves adorning, wired-on Nutz.
On this point, for this accessory, there's no debate.
So, let 'em dodge the gravel as they're lurching down the road.

Truck Nutz are standard automotive equipment for chip kickers,
And they adorn and accessorize hitches in rodeo parking lots,
But they would seem ghastly crude to city slickers,
And draw snickers from spectators as Truck Nutz go parading by.

Old Truck Nutz never die but they can, tragically, become disconnected,
After being pelted with rocks, stones, and clods that are hard.
Their departure and liberation may be unnoticed and quite unexpected,
As they suffer the ignominious fate of bouncing,
        untethered, down the boulevard.

Methuselas

If you peruse the obituaries in the local rag,
It would seem that poor people and people of color rarely die.
What a strange social and religious mixed bag,
To have these wonderful modern Methuselas, but why?

How wonderful to pay respects in print
And read about the life of the deceased
At a time of mourning and deep lament.
It's a fitting tribute to lost friends and kinfolks.

We get to read about all of the maw maws
And lovely nannas and memaws.
Don't forget the peepaws and paw paws,
Who are frequently mentioned in the obits.

But in the obits, people are rarely reported as "dying."
Instead, they "go to live with angels,"
Or "get their wings:" Mystifying.
Many obits also report they "returned to their heavenly home."

Unfortunately, we rarely get to read about "going home,"
By poor people or people of color.
Methuselas seem to be destine to forever roam
Because their departures rarely appear in print.

Methinks the rub of this inadvertent dissing by omission
Is the lack of sufficient scratch
To pay the newspaper the required remuneration
To document the Methusela's heavenly dispatch.

The Obtuse Goose

A terrible avian virus was on the loose
And sickening the flock
Of every gander and goose
And could destroy all the feathered honkers.

The virus could be the goose flu
Or the deadly fowl pox.
Whatever it was, the birds didn't know what to do.
So, they pecked at each other as the virus grew.

A golden medical vaxx was offered to the flock
But an obtuse and defiant goose
Decided to resist and balk,
Insisting the vaxx was a conspiracy of medical misuse.

The obtuse goose quickly emerged in the flock,
And vociferously and curmudgeonly
Said the vaxx was just poppycock.
And the geese in the gaggle kept on dying.

This vaxx would make a goose sterile and mutant,
And it contained a microchip, he said,
That would allow the go'ment to spy with evil intent.
And, the dead geese kept being thrown in the burning pit.

So, if there's an obtuse goose
Spewing nonsense and on the loose,
Ignore this quack, hoodoo, hocus-pocus honker
And follow scientific medical use.

WTH Does It Mean?

There's a new flurry of colloquialisms going around.
On first inspection and analysis, it would seem
Some appear quite logical and profound,
But it's very hard to tell what they actually mean.

Some expressions are trite and overused,
And pure jabber that leaves the keen listener
More perplexed and confused,
And sometimes, conned by verbal effluent.

Does "He couldn't get his head wrapped around it,"
Have a sensible and clear meaning?
It sems to be a declaration for a nitwit
And a case of blatant gibberishing.

What about, "She was comfortable in her own skin?"
This seems more like petty pretentious prattle
With very little sanity and clarity therein,
That crassly provides the listener with abject ambiguity.

All this hogwash can "Blow your mind,"
Fog and "Gaslight" the conversation,
And "Freak you out," unless you can deduce or find
What the hell it means.

Portable Thrones

How wonderful the invention
Of a place to go when you're on the go.
But there's no masking your intention
When you use a portable fiberglass outhouse.

Alas, how painful it is for others to see
The agony and stress on your face
While waiting in line to pee
And holding it until your turn at a *Portable Throne*.

When you get the urge and your stomach is in a knot,
How grateful and relieved you are to see
A row of *Johnnies-on-the-Spot*,
And many of the doors signaling "empty."

If you are using a *Stop and Go Potty*
At an outdoor fair or music concert,
The beat of the music will be more desiderate
As it vibrates the fiberglass potty walls.

You can pop into a *Porta-Loo* with delight
And take advantage of the facilities
At a local construction site
And hope the facility isn't moved during your visit.

Beware, though, when you visit a *Spiffy Biff*,
You might need to hold your nose
So that you don't get a big whiff
Of a potty not recently sanitized.

Sadly, if you use a *Honey Bucket* with urgency
You may get caught without paper
And suffer a *Porta Potty* emergency,
And no one to call for assistance.

So, enjoy the use of a *Chem Can*
If a convenience or emergency arises
And be glad you're not the service man
That cleans the *Rolling Throne* devices.

Not Going Back

We're not going back to using items we previously demanded
That have become obsolete or antique, to our dismay.
Ironically, we enjoyed, depended on, and took them for granted
Not so far back in the day

Though it used to be very cool tool
For making a manual calculation,
We're not going back to using a slide rule
That has suffered an unceremonious extinction.

Unfortunately, if you need a phone booth
To have an important conversation,
You are out of luck and must be long in the tooth.
Alas, we're not going back to booth communication.

If you need a slide or overhead projector,
You're in a technological pickle
Because they're not being used by an educator
And they're not worth a plug nickel.

Woe to the person who needs a rolodex
To keep an inventory of numbers, names and places
Because it is one of many extinct office objex
And we're not going back to the relic on any basis.

Furthermore, we're not returning to paper maps.
They've become obsolete, even for the devout
Because GPS and other apps
Help us find a location and a route.

You won't find encyclopedias on the living room floor.
They've become an archaic dead weight,
Coffee table and thrift store décor,
And a tome full of information that is out-of-date.

We said good-by to the rotary phone
Many phone models in the past.
Where they all went is unknown,
Replaced by the cell phone quite fast.

Film used to come in a roll,
Which we popped into a camera for a while.
Well, we're not going back to a photographic droll
When we have cameras on cell phones that are mobile.

Whether it's floppy disks, 8 tracks, or CDs,
We're not going back to gadgets, widgets, and earlier tech.
The landfills are full of old tech that was once the bee's knees
So, beware, your gas engine could soon be gone, what the heck.

Robocalls

Well, robocalls irk us in the morning,
Terrorize us in the evening,
And at suppertime and bedtime.
For heaven's sake, stop the irksome calls
And leave us alone all the time.

You can put your phone under your pillows
And swear at the robo callers,
But you're doomed to be irked forever
By the techno hard ballers
Who send the annoying rings coming in billows.

Now, robocalls can come anytime
To disturb your peaceful quiet zone,
And cause you to scream at the ether,
And cause you to curse and vilify your phone.
It seems we've created a techno torturer.

Landline or cell,
These unwanted solicitors
Have created a communications hell.
Now, the devil is SPAM
And a malicious phone scam inquisitor.

Gym Rats

Gyms and fitness clubs usually contain members of different types.
These gym rats tend to have eccentric personalities
As they try to win their fitness stripes.
What you see in the parodies has some basis in social realities.

The usual type of gym rat is into bodybuilding,
And they're less about strength than about appearance
Which is very ostentatious, and to us, quite bewildering,
As they flex and pose in the mirror with dogged perseverance.

Another type of rat is the Howler in the gym.
This fanatic believes in making crude animal-like sounds.
His silly noises mean you will hear him before you spot him
As he lifts heavy weights of many pounds.

In the gym, the Slob is hard to miss.
This rat never wipes down the equipment, without regret,
Leaves weights and dumbbells quite amiss,
Does not wear deodorant, and is dripping with sweat.

The gym Fashionista wears the latest fitness fashion
And in front of the mirror, spends most of her time
Because exercising is not her true passion
And sweating would be a fashionista crime.

It is hard to miss the gym rat Mixer
Who carries his own shaker bottle and cup
Filled with ample amounts of powdered fitness elixir
That, hopefully, won't lead to a gym floor cleanup.

The gym rat Hoarder is a complete boor,
Carries many items around the gym, by all means,
Scatters water bottles and bag items all over the floor,
Including the area around the strength machines.

For the Gear gym rat, gear is one of his first loves.
He carries compression gear and lifting straps,
Knee wraps and workout gloves
And hogs the equipment for sets and reps.

It's sad to see the Depressed gym man.
He works out because his wife or physician
Has forced him out of the bar and into a gym plan
Because of his deplorable physical condition.

The Tough Guys strut and parade around the gym floor
Like they're in a brash, belligerent, badass dream.
They slam weights, grunt, and swear with a roar
As they take their toughness to the extreme.

Just about all gym rats wear buds in their ears.
The Singer listens to the music and sings aloud along
So that everyone suffers and hears,
And sees this rat dance to their favorite song.

Some gym rat types fit a mold quite well
But anyone who makes the effort should get credit
For not being the couch potato from hell.
It's not easy but they can say they did it.

Gimme Somma That!

There seems to be an abundance of meds
Available to cure what afflicts and ails us,
Energize our bodies, calm our tormented heads,
And leave us with drugs that are superfluous.
So, gimme s'more!

Alas, if you suffer from kneemonia,
You can, mercifully, take *Tremfoya*
That will make you feel like a spring petunia.
And, the maker says there's nothing better for ya.
So, you need to get somma that!

Furthermore, if you contract toemain,
You need to be treated with *Ombrelvy*
To alleviate your suffering and pain,
And continue to live splendidly,
If you get somma that.

Fortunately, if you are afflicted with thighroidism,
You can quickly take *Ozempick,*
So that you can return to a healthy optimism.
The medicine will do the trick,
After you get some of that.

Woefully, the pain of chingles can be intense,
But if you religiously take some *Breastry,*
Your recovery will be immense,
And you will be feeling spry, by and by.
So, you'll be glad you got some of that.

If you suffer from a hiptheria ailment,
Take some prescribed *Trulicitee,*
So that you can realize peace and contentment,
And you hip will be sitting pretty
After you take some of that.

What an amazing selection of miracle meds available
To treat many terrible afflictions
To keep us healthy, safe, and able
By taking advantage of drug interdictions.
Gimme somma that!

Packets

One of the latest restaurant rackets
Is a small individual portion
Served in a paper or plastic packet
By zipping open the enclosures for custom apportion.

Gone are the unsanitary bottles, jars, or tubs
Sitting on the restaurant tables or trays
That could lead to messy flubs
Of the contents all over dining buffets.

No more salt and pepper shakers,
Catsup, mustard, or mayonnaise
For salad or sandwich makers
Who can easily open a packet, now-a-days.

Forget zip-lock and shrink wrap: They can't hack it.
Dispense your salad dressing, hot sauce, and parmesan cheese
In a convenient one-time portion packet
And your dining will be a condiment and culinary breeze.

Gone is the squishy squeeze bottle rocket
And explosive pump dispenser messes.
A handful of packets can go home in a purse or pocket
For home condiment excesses.

Forget the cryogenic freezing, embalming, and cremation.
Just puree me for all time's sake
And bury me in a bunch of packets for salvation,
My soul the Lord to keep.

Batteryfication

We seemed to be swamped with electronic devices
That have overwhelmed our normal existence
And require a deluge of batteries for activation.
Looks like we are undergoing a complete batteryfication
And creating electronic codependency and coexistence.

We fiddle and fumble with insertable
Cs, Ds, AAs, AAAs, and Ns,
Whose sizes are not substitutable
And don't fit when you need 'em.
Beware, this battery invasion may be insurmountable.

Batteries run our clocks, alarms, flashlights, and smoke detectors,
So that we live with a recycling and recharging specter.
They also drive our tooth brushes, watches, and shavers.
Are we are being covered in a tsunami of microchips
Contained in these modern, energizer driven, labor savers?

Where would we be without batteries
In our toys, games, and mobile phones
To keep everything charged and in sync?
We watch it all with our battery powered drones
And we batteryfy everything but the kitchen sink.

Alas, we also have the very modern and chic
Battery operated toilets and tissue dispensers.
But you are electronically potty-up-the-creek
If the battery loses its charge and dies
Or there's a malfunction of the sensors.

How wonderful it is that batteryfication allows us
To ride on scooters and skateboards and in our e-cars and golf carts,
Wearing our battery powered hearing aids and pacemakers,
While checking our vital signs with our fit watches, with much fuss,
Hoping we have enough batteries to operate our faulty body.

IQ Agua Fria

We can now drink bottled water
That will raise your IQ
And make you a lot smarter.
It will quench a thirst for you,
This bottled agua fria.

But, are you smarter for buying the water in plastic
Or, does the water make you smarter?
Seems the claims are quite fantastic
And the health benefits a nonstarter,
For this bottled agua fria.

The bottled water comes from Britain, France, and Norway
And as far away as the Fiji Islands.
It comes sparkling, mineral, or purified in some way.
The best may come from the Arkansas highlands,
And is mountain spring agua fria.

If you like your water deionized
Or treated by reverse osmosis,
Drink bottled water as advertised
To help you with your hidrosis.
Bottled agua fria is the trendiest.

For me, smart bottled water ain't my thing.
There's too much plastic in the sea,
So, give me some dumb water out of the tap or a spring
To eliminate all of the plastic debris
By drinking agua fria that is plastic free.

Pet Psymeds

We now have prescription and OTC psymeds for a pet
That can alter their mood and behavior,
So that our fur babies and owners no longer need to fret
And the human-animal bond becomes stronger.

Don't let your precious Pekinese tremble and quiver
When there is lightning and thunder.
Feed him some *Woofium*
And he will no longer run asunder.

If your Great Dane
Isn't feeling so great,
Slip him some *Zolofur* for his pain,
And he won't hesitate.

When your perky poodle dog
Is under the weather,
Give her some *Pawbutrin*
And you two can now hang together.

If your pit bull is agitated,
And shaking and pacing,
Give him some *Pupulti*
And his strong heart will stop racing.

So, if your pampered pup
Is on a spectrum
Give him some *Barkadril*
By inserting it into his rectum.

If your loveable Labrador lap dog
Shows symptoms of PTSD,
You might want to put some *Howlassin* in his food,
So that he becomes more relaxed and symptom free.

If your loveable pet is a Chihuahua
Who exhibits ADHD from time to time,
He might need a minimum dose of *Tigeanol*
To return him to his doggie prime.

Caution: Giving meds to your pet
Could cause them to be sick or addicted.
So, before you get an OTC or prescription,
Check with your vet to see if your pet is emotionally afflicted.

Historical

Ballad of the Canary of the Brazos

Some people said she was a beautiful raven-haired Louisiana belle.
Others said she was a black creole witch from hell.
She came up a Texas river on a small steamer boat
With her blue-eyed son, a little voodoo, and a wool army coat.

The Canary sang and died on the "River of the Arms of God."

She sang nightly in the Napoleon Bar
And in the Crescent City, she was quite a star.
In N'awlins, this lady was free
But outside the city, from the slavers she had to flee.

The Canary sang and died on the "River of the Arms of God."

After a quarrel between two of her lovers ended in a deadly gunfight,
She fled to the wharf in the dark of night
To escape the wrath of the friends and relatives of her exes.
She welcomed a chance to semi-stowaway on a boat to Texas.

The Canary sang and died on the "River of the Arms of God."

Was she an Indian, Mexican, or slave?
Or a demon spirit from a swampy grave?
She knew her numbers and could read and write
And for a slave, being educated just wasn't right.

The Canary sang and died on the "River of the Arms of God."

The safety boys caught her at Port Sullivan and left her swinging.
But folks around these parts say they still hear her screaming and singing.
Late at night the Canary walks the banks of the Brazos River.
Now that old river specter makes momma's children shake and quiver.

The Canary sang and died on the "River of the Arms of God."

Juanna Mesteno

Sally Skull rode into Texas legends and history
On her horse Redbuck accompanied by her vaqueros.
Where she went is an enduring mystery,
But she left a trail of rich, bloody, mythical and gritty tales
Across South Texas frontier towns and trails.

She was the original "Mustang Sally,"
But her vaqueros called her Juanna Mesteno
Because her first name was originally Jane.
She came to Texas with the first families
Of Stephen F. Austin's colony inflow.

Sally acquired the last name Skull
From her second husband.
Married five times,
She killed at least two spouses
And her relationship with the others
Was violent and tempestuous, oftentimes.

Sally's piercing steel-blue eyes
Focused into the fixed stare of a hawk
When she met others and played poker.
Her complexion was dark, sun-leathered and rough.
The swearing she used was also rough and foul talk.

Mustang Jane spoke Spanish fluently
And did all the work of men, in a sense.
She loved to dance and drink at a fandango,
But she was quick to anger and violence,
And could use a whip, knife, or pistol as good as any gringo.

Even though she couldn't read or write,
She played high stakes poker,
And always carried a sack of gold
Secured to the horn of her hand tooled saddle
Which was trimmed in silver bright.

This notorious lady of the Wild Horse Desert
Helped keep the Confederacy alive.
With her wagon trains and herds of horses,
She sold cotton and horses to the Rebs
Along with guns, ammunition, and supplies, in concert.

She drove horses from Mexico and South Texas
North to the Nacogdoches town to make a deal
And hauled cotton south to Alleyton,
Bound for the Mexican port of Bagdad.
She was the queen of the Cotton Road and Camino Real.

When Sally was traversing the Cotton Road,
Her favorite outfit was a buckskin shirt, tailored to a T.
Her jacket and bright red flannel clearly showed
And her sunbonnet was the only sign of femininity
When she was riding the trail.

Her ever-present French pistols
Were always hidden in the folds of her skirt
When she wasn't sporting six shooters.
She was a femme fatale that could make a man hurt,
With a reputation for doing-in husbands.

Some describe her as a merciless killer
When she was aroused and willing
And it didn't take much to arouse her.
She decided who needed killing
And obliged those hapless men she didn't like.

This lady who was notorious for her husbands,
Horse trading and equine artistry,
Freighting, roughness, brigands,
Champion cussing and card playing,
Disappeared and rode her horse into history.

Klan Kostume In the Kloset

Beau and Maybelle have a historical artifact hidden in the Kloset.
It is a Klan hood and robe that her great grandfather wore to rallies.
The costume has been in the family since long ago,
And they don't want anybody to know it's there.
They especially don't want the grandchildren to know,
But the children know the Klan Kostume is in the Kloset.

Adult children who know asked Maybelle about the Kloset.
Jokingly she said, "Being in the Klan was as Southern
        as grits and pecan pie:
It was all white and full of nuts."
But ambivalently, she also said, "If my neighbors found out,
I declare, I'd just die." She mustn't let on about the lie.
So, decidedly, the Klan Kostume remains in the Kloset.

On other occasions, Beau and Maybelle
Asserted that the Kostume was a cultural icon, in fact,
And part of a great and glorious southern heritage.
They expressed pride in Maybell's great grandfather
And declared his ensemble was a valuable historical artifact.
So, the prized Klan Kostume hangs in the Kloset.

The curious grandchildren inquired
About this most public private artifact in town.
Maybelle said it was an old choir gown.
So, three generations have guarded this sacred but undesired,
Ghostly, anachronistic, repulsive, and white artifact
That stays forever and religiously hidden in the Kloset.

Fire On the Wall

The "Grape" rolled effortlessly down I-25,
The purplish-gray shadows of the eastern slope to the right,
And the lights of Denver in the rear view.
The radio was playing the latest "Beetles" jive,
But thoughts and intentions were about making it
To Amarillo by evening and the dark of night.

The Grape's name had begun as the "Grape Mobile."
It was the only wheels available for the entire staff,
And they initially gave the shortened name, semi-on the sly,
To the wine colored, 1963, Delta 88 Oldsmobile
That served as the staff tour bus, taxi,
And excursion van to enjoy a Rocky Mountain high.

Final checkout at J-Mac had been four o'clock,
So, beginning the drive down the freeway was late.
Final exams for the spring quarter were over, mercifully,
But the events of the previous nine months were swirling
In my head like driving and sleepwalking, simultaneously,
As the Grape headed us to a new fate.

Thank gawd, no more pink, green, blue, and yellow forms,
Late night dreary typing of damage and incident reports,
Boring classes, incessant staff meetings,
And interpersonal conflicts among the staff consorts.
In addition, there would be no more cross-campus trips to deliver
Reports through driving snow storms.

The gas gage on the Grape showed only half
As the macabre incidents of the last nine months
Punctuated the deserted road in the dark.
Seeing roadside scenes and miles of chaff,
And mulling other thoughts left me numb and mesmerized,
And looking for an idyllic roadside park.

There were harbingers of events on campus in the sixties.
From campus activities and world events,
To the coffee shop and street hippie scene,
Unrest and social protest were in the air.
Periodic chaotic food fights and food riots, trashing the cuisine,
Left dining in J-Mac a nauseating and tense affair.

Riots and demonstrations, large and small
 Occurred routinely on Thursday nights.
What they were about was not clear at all,
But most seemed to be about the war in "Nam" and civil rights.
A tuition increase led to a burning of the books
In protest on the university athletic field.

Passing through Pueblo and heading for Trinidad,
Led to recollecting the vision in my mind of the discovery
Of a room of fecal covered St. Bernard pups in a litter,
Which was reeking of doggie odors: cute but sad and bad.
The pungent doggie dorm room debacle
Led to a three carbon, three-page typing twitter.

Heading to Amarillo by way of Raton Pass
Brought back memories of each day's
Extensive incident and damage reports
That were all, at this time, a visionary morass:
Prostitutes in the rooms, flooded hallways,
And a complete engine repair shop in J-Mac.

In the Fall of '63, the residents of J-Mac,
After a riot, began to drift back to the hall,
And after the police and fire hoses restored civility
 At the corner of East Evans and South High Street.
They were still agitated and excited, after all,
And well after the unruly, riotous, and violent activity.

Cruising through Amarillo on the dark plain,
Scenes flooded back vividly and unexpectedly.
The call came from the resident assistant of the bottom floor domain.

He frantically indicated that J-Mac was on fire,
That I needed to come now, and he had called the fire department
Because the blazing situation was dire.

The entire external wall of the three-story building was in flames
And resembled a surreal Dantean scene
As burning bed sheets cascaded down the wall
And caught on the cranked-out casement windows
After bedclothes had been soaked in kerosene.
They hung burning, illuminating both external walls of the residence hall.

The patio between the wings of the hall was now smokey and dark
Except for the flickering charred embers on the ground.
It had been an existential and occupational event
That was pivotal, insightful, and profound.
The fire hoses were retrieved and rolled up
And stowed back on the truck after inaction.
It was now clear the Grape and the career
Needed to go in a different academic direction.

Left Wichita Falls in the dark headed for Dallas on the US 287 road
And started nodding off and veering the Grape to the shoulder,
Indicating I wasn't able to focus on driving at all.
No more flashbacks about the wretched J-Mac abode
And memories of uber-tension and Fire On the Wall
Because I stopped the Grape at 5 a.m. in a roadside park and fell asleep.

Fire In the Pines

The gov'ment man went to Dodge Station
To notify Lil Cute's daddy
He had to fight in the Great War for the nation.
He said no: He had seven mouths to feed.

Lil Cute and her sisters and brothers, Tenola, Bessie, Thomas, and Pete.
Lived in a one-room, flitch board cabin,
Without a well, electricity, or heat.
Believe, mama Sarah guarded her precious brood.

Lil Cute always wore a lavender dress that was a hand-me-down.
She treasured it and rarely took it off even though it was outgrown.
It was a gift from Sara's boss lady in the town.
And, it was the only dress Lil Cute would ever own.

Daddy George worked at a local saw mill,
Stacking heavy lumber from the cut pine logs.
Mama Sarah worked toiling at an antebellum mansion on a hill,
After walking ten miles to the prison town.

With barefooted Cute, Tenola, and Bessie in tow,
They left the cabin before sunrise and returned after dark.
They went when the cold wind would blow,
And, rain or shine, cold or hot, down the sandy road they would embark.

The gov'ment man took umbrage at George's uppitiness and belligerence,
And told the sheriff in the prison town.
The two agreed that George needed to be arrested for public assurance.
So, the word was spread that George was a bellicose troublemaker
    and violent threat.

Rumors zipped through the town that a posse was being organized.
Armed men were needed for an impending gunfight,
And volunteers would be furnished guns and deputized.
Quickly, the citizens became tight-lipped and fearful
    about the impending violent night.

Soon after midnight, twenty wagons of armed men left the state pen,
    torches burning bright.
They rode stealthily on wagons usually ridden by chained men,
On their way to Dodge Station this moonless night.
So, in a line, mules dutifully and stoically pulled
    the clandestine ragtag lawmen.

The gray tree trunks were illuminated by the Dantean torch light,
As the fiery caravan snaked through the pine forest.
The bristling guns signaled that these men were ready to fight.
And, ominously, there was going to be blood on the pine straw tonight.

The smell of burning pitch cut through the humid night air of June,
As the smoke from the torches waffed through the tall conifers,
And the men listened to the familiar staccato tune
Of mules rattling and jangling the binding singletrees and traces.

Each deputy, with excitement and apprehension, tightly held his rifle.
Most had chugged spirits before leaving and they were feeling scrappy.
But each hoped it wasn't going to be a fool's errand or a midnight trifle.
Tragically, it was a perfect situation for someone to get trigger happy.

Even though all were fully deputized,
Most had never killed a man.
But, the fear in their eyes was fully realized,
When the pace of the mules quickened as they got closer.

The posse crossed the railroad tracks and traveled a short distance,
Where they saw the faint glow of oil lamps in a cabin.
Assembling in rifle shot distance, there wasn't any immediate resistance.
It was very quiet as the light from the torches reflected from the cabin.

Some of the deputies had puzzled looks on their faces,
Because the cabin looked so small and unmenacing for such a large force.
They were incredulous that such large threats could be in such small places.
Superficially, none wanted to look scared and craven.

A rifle shot flashed and cracked through the night
And broke the eerie charged silence.
Each deputy's gun was loaded and had the cabin in the gunsight.
Quickly, a barrage of gunfire erupted
      and riddled the walls of the small cabin.

The pierced cabin walls were splintered and scarred
And the windows shattered into twinkling chards.
The front door fell from its hinges and into the front yard.
The cabin began to lean when the supports were weakened.

The cabin began to flicker and burn.
Sara dragged her son Pete to the front porch
And was immediately killed in turn.
The structure was soon engulfed in flames and a complete immolation.

The flames from the large macabre blaze
Rose high in the sky, scorching the green pine needles.
The roof fell in, and sparks burst upward from the smokey haze.
The stunned deputies stared transfixed at the fire in the pines.

To escape the deadly pyre,
Lil Cute crawled into the backyard.
Her hair was gone as well as her lavender attire.
Screaming, she collapsed on the forest floor.

She screamed and screamed,
Whimpered and screamed some more.
Then she died, her soul redeemed
Alone, in the dark, under the tall pine trees.

The wagons disappeared into the night
After the torches were extinguished.
It hadn't been much of a gunfight.
And now, the whole family had vanished.

Over a hundred years of fallen pine straw covers the site
And hides the acrid sooty smell of burnt pitch pine,
And the cabin where an entire family was burned to death one night.
All that is left is the sweet smell of the lavender wisteria vines.

Listen and you can hear
Lil Cute screaming in the pines
When the wind rustles
The lavender wisteria vines.

Pledges

The light from the roaring and crackling flames
Danced across and reflected off the concrete support beams
Underneath the bridge that sheltered the informal initiation site,
As the nude pledges prepared for late night degrading antics and games.

Their glistening painted sticky red bodies
Glowed with a sheen in the firelight
And smelled of freshly applied enamel paint on the newbies,
As they huddled apprehensively in the Dantean night.

The acrid smoke from the blaze
Rose in the air and hovered over the scene,
And created a other worldly haze
As it settled over the clandestine gathering under the bridge.

The members were giddy with eagerness and delight
As they prepared to depredate the victims waiting by the flames,
Shouting and calling them revolting, debasing, and scatological names
At this secret, but very public, unauthorized assembly late at night.

The paddle bloodied and bruised cheeks held a wiener they must not expel,
As the wide-eyed and frightened flock ran through the dust
To deposit the red dogs in a container, but if the wiener fell,
They had to start over after eating it with a little dusty crust.

They retched and heaved after they drank the putrid pledge tea,
And became hazy and dazed after quick-drying glue
    was smeared in all body hair.
After the fire was extinguished, the members, guffawing, left with esprit.
Without their prey, they rode miles back to town
    after the abhorrent affair.

They had acted out the traditional frat hiatus and educational pause
For the ghoulish, informal, and annual rite,
Revealing the macabre psychological and motivational flaw
Of white American frat brats on pledge initiation night.

Bediasites

Thirty-six million years ago,
  A streaking, burning, and arcing
    Meteor hit Chesapeake Bay,
      Formed a watery crater,
        And created a strewn zone
          Of impact fusion glass.
            Found today,
              These Texas tektites
                Now abound
                  In central Texas
                    On the ground,
                      As bulldozers pass
                        And uncover
                          Little bits of
                            Black glass
                              That are a
                                Quite scarce
                                  Tektite,
                                    A geological
                                      Curiosity,
                                        And a
                                          Rock
                                            Hunters
                                              Delight.

Mythical

The Twisted Cryptid

Peering out from behind a mesquite thicket
Could be a lurking wily Chupacabra.
This monster ain't no ordinary thicket cricket,
But could be an elusive twisted cryptid.

The mythical chupa haunts the wild horse desert
Vampireishly killing sheep, goats, and chickens,
Which leaves the locals with eerie disconcert
Because, poof, the elusive cryptid quickly disappears.

Some say it's a wolf, wild dog, or coyote
That is sick, scraggly, and scruffy.
Others say it's a vision from ingesting peyote.
Whatever, this cryptid critter is a sneaky and shifty toughie.

So, if you're ever in south Texas, take care,
And beware of the blood sucking Chupacabra
That prowls the prairies, arroyos, and thickets there.
Warning: This critter is a very twisted cryptid.

The Dinosaur's Lament

With a raptorial toothy grin,
The Blancasaurus looked up
To the cretaceous sky
And saw the ne'er seen tail
Of a meteor streaking by.

He wasn't moved or frightened
By such a cosmic event
Because he enjoyed
Eternal supremacy
And ruled with perfect indemnity.

Even with a blinding flash of light
And impending darkness and extinction,
He still thought he had more time.
He had enjoyed power and dominance
For so long, so he assumed he would tonight.

Dark clouds of dust fell over his domain,
So, he screeched and roared a mighty wail,
And gnashed his dagger teeth in refrain.
It was the freezing Blancasaurus's
And all the other dino's dying song, of little avail.

After the cataclysmic blast, darkness,
Iridium snow, and perpetual cold,
Small free mammalian creatures were ravenous
And fed on the carcass of the rotting beast,
And enjoyed the abundance of the cretaceous feast.

Cryocryptids

As the polar ice melts away,
Many frozen creatures are being exposed,
Because for millions of years there has not been any decay.
Now, new possibilities are being posed.

What if a mythical cryptid creature is exposed?
Bigfoot could come out of the ice
And be freed from his long repose.
Wouldn't that be a DNA paradise?

We could see a sasquatch up close and real,
And photograph and study the hairy beast.
Wouldn't that be an anthropological reveal,
To see a cryptid that lived thousands of years ago?

Nessie might be on display
For all cryptid hunters to see and gawk,
Forever freed from her frozen lake way.
How thrilling it would be to see a monster from the lock.

Fortuitously, we might get to finally see a kraken
If one appears from beneath the ice.
If all of the other frozen cryptids begin to awaken,
We might, eventually, have a thawed zoo of cryptid monsters.

The San Juan River Monster

Watch out boys for that toothy ole river monster.
It lurks on the San Juan River and the fork to the east.
Folks say it's half bear, half man.
So, boys kill the monster if you can,
Or you might become the strange monster's feast.
Also, if you travel on the San Juan stream
And hear a deadly scream, keep your powder dry
And behind you a watchful eye,
Because the monster will your death deem.

The monster has been seen under the Apache Street bridge
Catching, skinning and eating a trout fish.
And, has appeared up on Piedra ridge,
Under the Palisades on the East Fork,
And there have been several sightings up on the divide.
Strangely, the elk hunters never see him
And nobody seems to know
When and where he will appear,
Or where he does reside.

With the head of a bear
And the body of a man,
You'll get a chilling and eerie scare
From this clawed and toothy monster,
Who roams the San Juan River valley.
He will leave a deer or elk carcass
Hanging in a tree or on a fence post
After he strikes in the darkness,
This San Juan River man-ghost.

Legend has it that the beast
Emerged from the big hot spring,
A bizarre creature from the underworld,
Forever to roam the San Juan valley
As an outcast and abominated being.

Attracted to the fumaroles in winter,
And driven to the high meadows in summer,
He is elusive and seclusive, avoiding a town center,
This sulfurous beast from the big hot spring.

Surely, visit the San Juan River,
Tube the rapids, take a hike,
And sit in the warm waters of the springs.
Also, enjoy the alpine serenity, if you like,
And the thrill a wildlife sighting brings.
Above all, avoid late night visits
To a fishy smelling garbage dumpster
Because your fellow snooper and diver
Could be a bear or the San Juan River Monster.

The Bedias Beast

Watch out floaters and boaters for the river beast.
It lurks on the Navasota River and creeks to the east.
Folks say it's half gator, half man.
So, avoid the beast if you can,
Or you might become the beast's feast.
Also, if you travel on the Navasota stream
And hear a deadly howl or scream,
Keep a wary and watchful eye
Because the beast will your death deem.

The beast has been seen at Hidalgo Falls on the prowl,
On the upper reaches of Bedias and Panther Creeks,
And at Piedmont Hot Springs in the winter,
And several people around Iola, Reliance, and North Zulch
Have heard his terrifying and piercing yowl.
Strangely, deer and hog hunters never see him
And nobody seems to know
When and where he will appear
Or where this zoomorphic creature seems to go.

With the head of an alligator
And the body of a man,
You'll get a chilling and eerie scare
From this black clawed and toothy beast
Who roams, standing upright, the Bedias region.
Sometimes on a violent tear,
He smashes rowboats and outbuildings
When he appears, strikes, and rampages at night,
This ferocious crocodilian beast.

Legend has it that the tormented sole
Emerged from the Piedmont Hot Springs
High over the Navasota River's ridge to the east,
A bizarre cryptid creature from a spewing fumarole,
Forever roaming as an outcast and abominated being.

Attracted to the hot spring during the chill of winter,
And driven by the insects to the high ridges in summer,
He is elusive and seclusive, avoiding a town center,
This odorous and sulfurous beast of the Bedias.

Surely, fish in the Bedias Creek,
Catch some crappie and bass,
And sit down to a scaly feast.
Enjoy the rural serenity, if you wish
And the thrill a fish fry brings.
Above all, watch for late night visits by varmints
Attracted to the odors of frying fish,
Because an unexpected dinner guest
Could be the ferocious Bedias Beast.

About the Author

Robert A. Shearer is retired Professor of Criminal Justice at Sam Houston State University. As a professor, in addition to teaching graduate and undergraduate courses, he served as a consultant to many county, state, and federal Criminal Justice agencies. He published extensively, and is often cited in numerous Criminal Justice publications.

He is now one of the predominant faculty members of CEUMATRIX-The Institute for Addictions and Criminal Justice Studies. Thousands of students have completed his on-line courses for substance abuse counselor certification. He is a member of the Citizen Potawatomi Nation of Oklahoma. He is currently an avid writer and e-bike cyclist.

Printed in the USA
CPSIA information can be obtained
at www.ICGtesting.com
LVHW050432080924
790167LV00002B/7

9 781622 889525